How to deal with DISCRIMINATION

Rachel Lynette

PowerKiDS press™

New York

Published in 2009 by The Rosen Publishing Group, Inc.
29 East 21st Street, New York, NY 10010

First Edition

Editor: Joanne Randolph
Book Design: Kate Laczynski
Photo Researcher: Jessica Gerweck

Photo Credits: Cover, p. 1 © www.iStockphoto.com/Jamie Wilson; p. 4 © www.iStockphoto.com/Ana Abejon; p. 6 © SuperStock/Age Fotostock; p. 8 Shutterstock.com; p. 10 © Don Smetzer/Getty Images; p. 12 © Fat Chance Productions/Getty Images; p. 14 © www.iStockphoto.com/Cliff Parnell; p. 16 © Stephen Simpson/Getty Images; p. 18 © www.iStockphoto.com/Thomas Gordon; p. 20 © www.iStockphoto.com/Bonnie Jacobs.

Library of Congress Cataloging-in-Publication Data

Lynette, Rachel.
  How to deal with discrimination / Rachel Lynette. — 1st ed.
      p. cm. — (Let's work it out)
  Includes index.
  ISBN 978-1-4042-4518-1 (library binding)
  1. Discrimination—Juvenile literature. I. Title.
  HM821.L95 2009
  177'.5—dc22

                                        2008007140

Manufactured in the United States of America

Contents

What Is Discrimination? 5

Different Kinds of Discrimination 7

Why Do People Discriminate? 9

Treating People Fairly 11

Being Discriminated Against 13

Discriminating Against Others 15

Another Point of View 17

Learning About Differences 19

More Alike than Different........................21

Celebrating Differences..........................22

Glossary 23

Index..24

Web Sites 24

14.99

Being mean to people who are different from you is wrong. Think about how you would feel if someone discriminated against you.

What Is Discrimination?

Some boys were playing kickball at recess. Sarah wanted to play, too. When she asked if she could play, Kyle said that only boys could play. Do you think Kyle treated Sarah fairly?

Discrimination is treating people badly or unfairly because they are different. It is never okay to treat people badly just because they are different from you. Discrimination can hurt people's feelings. It can also cause children to be made fun of or left out. Sometimes, discrimination can even lead to someone getting hurt.

These boys thought girls were not good at science. Soon they were glad to have Lisa in their study group, though.

Different Kinds of Discrimination

People are different in many different ways, so there are many kinds of discrimination. People may be different because they belong to different **ethnic groups**. African Americans, Latin Americans, Asians, and Caucasians are examples of different ethnic groups. Some people do not like people from other ethnic groups. This is called **racism**.

People can be discriminated against for other reasons, too. Women are sometimes discriminated against. People may also be discriminated against for their **religious** beliefs. People who are old, young, **disabled**, overweight, or sick may also be **victims** of discrimination.

It is hard to be prejudiced if you take the time to get to know people. These girls know that prejudiced people miss out on great friendships.

Why Do People Discriminate?

Tyler heard his grandfather say that Latinos are lazy. Tyler thought about his friend Carlos. Carlos was Latino, but he was not lazy. Tyler decided that his grandfather must be wrong about Latinos.

Not everybody thinks about what they hear the way Tyler did. Sometimes, people believe things about a person or a group of people without getting to know them. That is called **prejudice**.

People may also become prejudiced because they are afraid. People are sometimes afraid of people who are different from themselves. When people are prejudiced, they are likely to act on their feelings by discriminating.

Mike used to get left out a lot because he is in a wheelchair. Juan found out that Mike is a lot of fun, and now they play all the time.

Treating People Fairly

You will meet many different people in your life. Some you will like more than others. Get to know people before you decide how you feel about them. This will make you less likely to be prejudiced toward people. No matter how you feel about someone, it is important to treat that person fairly.

Treating someone fairly means not discriminating. Never call someone a name or tease him because he is different from you. When you play a game, make sure everyone is allowed to play. Try to treat everyone with kindness. Can you think of more ways to treat people fairly?

Being treated unfairly because of your skin color, or for any other reason, hurts. Talking to someone about how you feel can help.

Being Discriminated Against

If someone discriminates against you, you may feel **confused**, sad, or angry. You may be scared that the person will hurt you. It may help to remember that discrimination is always wrong. If you are discriminated against, it is not your fault.

If you are being bullied, try to tell the person to leave you alone. Walk away if you can. Never try to solve the problem by fighting. It is okay to ask for help. Talking to a trusted adult, like a parent, teacher, or **counselor** can help. Talking to your friends can help, too.

These boys used to treat Joseph unfairly. When they realized how bad they were making him feel, they knew it was time to stop.

Discriminating Against Others

If you are discriminating against another person, it is time to stop! Think about why you are treating that person unfairly. Do her differences scare you? Do you believe something about that person that may not be true? What can you do to change how you feel about that person?

One way to stop discriminating is to think about how your actions are hurting the other person. Are you making someone feel sad, left out, or afraid? You do not have to hurt other people. You can stop discriminating and start treating people fairly.

At first people were afraid to play with Aaron because he looked different. Soon, they learned he was great at sports and a good friend.

Another Point of View

At first Amber did not like Shanti. Shanti wore strange clothes and did not speak English very well. Sometimes, Amber and her friends made fun of Shanti's **accent**.

Then one day Amber saw Shanti crying by herself. Amber asked her what was wrong.

"I hate it here! No one likes me. I want to go back to India," Shanti said.

Amber thought about what it would be like to leave her home and move to a place where everyone was different. Amber felt bad about the way she had treated Shanti. Amber decided to be friends with Shanti.

By asking respectful questions, her classmates were able to learn a lot about Adila's Muslim beliefs.

Learning About Differences

You may feel prejudiced against someone because he is different from you. It can be helpful to talk about your differences. When you ask someone about a way in which he is different from you, it is important to be **polite** and respectful.

At first, Chris thought Jacob was strange because he always wore a little cap on his head. Then he asked Jacob about the cap. Jacob explained that he was Jewish and wearing the cap was part of his religion. It was called a yarmulke. Once Chris understood, he did not think it was strange at all!

Some girls on this team are tall, some are short, some are black, and some are white. They are different, but they all work together as a team.

More Alike than Different

One way to keep from discriminating against other people is to look for ways that you are the same. Jamal and Mario did not think they had anything in common. Then they discovered that they both like to play soccer. Now Jamal and Mario play soccer together almost every day!

Even though people can look different on the outside, people are often not so different on the inside. Everyone wants to be liked and respected. When you treat people with respect, you may find that you are not so different after all.

Celebrating Differences

Being with people who are different from you can be fun and exciting! You can learn many interesting things from people who are not like you. It can be fun to try new foods, learn about different **cultures**, and see things from someone else's point of view.

The next time you are around someone who is different from you, try to remember that on the inside you are probably more alike than different. If you treat that person with kindness instead of discriminating against her, you just might make a new friend!

Glossary

accent (AK-sent) The way a person from another country may pronounce English words.

confused (kun-FYOOZD) Mixed up.

counselor (KOWN-seh-ler) Someone who talks with people about their feelings and problems and who gives advice.

cultures (KUL-churz) The beliefs, practices, and arts of groups of people.

disabled (di-SAY-buld) Unable to do something.

discrimination (dis-krih-muh-NAY-shun) Treating a person badly or unfairly just because he or she is different.

ethnic groups (ETH-nik GROOPS) Groups of people who have the same race, beliefs, practices, or language, or who belong to the same country.

polite (puh-LYT) Behaving well in front of others.

prejudice (PREH-juh-dis) Disliking a group of people different from you.

racism (RAY-sih-zum) The belief that one group or race of people, such as whites, is better than another group, such as blacks.

religious (rih-LIH-jus) Having to do with a faith or a system of beliefs.

victims (VIK-timz) People or animals that are harmed or killed.

23

Index

E
ethnic groups, 7
examples, 7

F
fault, 13
feelings, 5, 9
friend(s), 9, 13, 17, 22

G
group, 9

K
kickball, 5
kindness, 11, 22

L
Latin Americans, 7
Latinos, 9
life, 11

P
prejudice, 9
problem, 13

R
racism, 7
reasons, 7
recess, 5
religious beliefs, 7

V
victims, 7

W
women, 7

Web Sites

Due to the changing nature of Internet links, PowerKids Press has developed an online list of Web sites related to the subject of this book. This site is updated regularly. Please use this link to access the list:
www.powerkidslinks.com/lwio/discrim/

24